Against Religion

CHATTO
CounterBlasts

A. N.

WILSON

Against Religion

Chatto & Windus
LONDON

Published in 1991 by
Chatto & Windus Ltd
20 Vauxhall Bridge Road
London SW1V 2SA

A CIP catalogue record for this book
is available from the British Library

ISBN 0 7011 3854 8

Photoset in Linotron Ehrhardt by
Rowland Phototypesetting Ltd
Bury St Edmunds, Suffolk
Printed in Great Britain by
St Edmundsbury Press Ltd
Bury St Edmunds, Suffolk

IT IS SAID in the Bible that the love of money is the root of all evil. It might be truer to say that the love of God is the root of all evil. Religion is the tragedy of mankind. It appeals to all that is noblest, purest, loftiest in the human spirit, and yet there scarcely exists a religion which has not been responsible for wars, tyrannies and the suppression of the truth. Marx described it as the opium of the people; but it is much deadlier than opium. It does not send people to sleep. It excites them to persecute one another, to exalt their own feelings and opinions above those of others, to claim for themselves a possession of the truth. If we read St Paul's famous hymn to Charity in his Epistle to the Corinthians, we see an incomparably exalted view of human virtue. 'Charity suffereth long, and is kind. Charity vaunteth not itself . . . rejoiceth not in iniquity, but rejoiceth in the truth.' When we consider the behaviour of the huge preponderance of religious people and religious organisations in the history of mankind, we come to realise that Religion is the precise opposite of what St Paul calls

I

Charity. Religion, far from suffering long, makes a point of establishing itself as the sole highway to salvation, and brooks no dissent from those who have the temerity to disagree with it. Religion is not kind; it is cruel. Religion does not rejoice in the truth. In fact, all the major religions go out of their way to suppress the truth and to label those who attempt to tell the truth as heretics. Religion vaunteth itself, is puffed up; but worse: by trying to bring good things to pass, it brings very evil things to pass. Like a human psychopath it is at war with all its own best instincts, because it knows, if these impulses were followed, it would destroy itself.

There will be many readers who already want to interrupt me and say, 'You must qualify what you have to say, by stating that you are only attacking false religion. "Pure religion and undefiled" can only lead to sweetness and light for the human race. We, as good Muslims, or good Catholics, or good Protestants, or good Hindus, would agree with you most earnestly that intolerance and cruelty and violence are a bad thing. But these things, which have been perpetrated in the name of religion, are the most terrible aberration. They are the result of human sin, not of religion. They are human qualities. Where religion is abolished, there is still no shortage of cruelty, persecution and war. Get rid

2

of religion, and you merely get rid of the highest ideals of the human race. Religion is the light to which we all aspire, the truth which we all seek, the union with God which is the greatest imaginable good for every individual human being.'

What I meant by saying that religion is the tragedy of mankind is that I cannot accept this point of view any longer. As someone who recognises strong religious impulses within himself, I used to rehearse this argument to myself again and again. Now that I have discarded any formal religious allegiance, I would not pretend to know what religion is, in the sense of knowing where it comes from, or whether it is to be accounted for by purely psychological explanations. But I do know, from the inside as well as from personal observation, that religion appeals to something deep and irrational and strong within us, and that this is what makes it so dangerous. If it were not so good, it would not be capable of being so bad. If it did not promise to make us good, promise to unite us to God Himself, it would not allow us the arrogance and self-righteousness which are its almost inevitable concomitants. There is a limit to human vanity and arrogance when it is confined to itself. If a man believes himself to be the wisest or strongest figure in the world, it would probably be impossible to puncture his vanity, or convince him that he might be wrong; but at least it would only be him that you were trying to puncture, his vanity, his arrogance, his self-conceit. It is very different when you are dealing with figures, such as Sir James Anderton, the Chief Constable of Greater Manchester, or Mrs Mary Whitehouse of the National Viewers and Listeners Association, who make no bones about being directly inspired by Almighty God. You can deflate purely human monsters. You cannot deflate God, even when He chooses to speak through such very peculiar mouthpieces as Mrs Whitehouse or Sir James Anderton. Still less can you deflate God when He speaks through the mouths of such exalted figures as an Ayatollah or a Pope.

In his message for the World Day of Peace on 3 February 1991, the Pope stated that, 'It is essential that the right to express one's own religious convictions publicly and in all domains of civil life be ensured if human beings are to live together in peace.' And, again, 'A serious threat to peace is posed by intolerance, which manifests itself in the denial of freedom of conscience to others. The excesses to which intolerance can lead has been one of history's most painful lessons.'

Presumably, when the Holy Father wrote these words, he had in mind the struggles for religious freedom in the Soviet Union and in the countries of the Warsaw Pact. He might also have been thinking of the declaration of the *fatwa* against Salman Rushdie (though it was interesting at the time when the Ayatollah Khomeini condemned Rushdie to death that the *Osservatore Romano* was one of the few journals in the civilised world to express solidarity with the Ayatollah's views).

Those within the bosom of the Catholic Church might find the Pope's plea for religious tolerance somewhat surprising. A little over a year ago, the Pope blocked the election of a blameless and much loved man to the Archbishopric of Cologne on the sole grounds that this bishop had dared to suggest that the moral questions surrounding birth control were not the most important facing the human race. He had not even advocated the use of contraception – he had merely questioned whether contraception was so important a matter as teaching people to be kind or to tell the truth. Catholic priests who do advocate the use of contraception have of course found themselves silenced or actually removed from office if they state their views publicly. In the Catholic universities of Europe, distinguished professors, such as Hans Küng have been deprived of their licenses to teach or lecture because they dared to question the doctrine of papal infallibility, or because they advocated a scholarly and open-minded approach to Biblical studies. All over Germany, and Holland and Spain and France and the United States, Catholics must be reading the Holy Father's plea for religious tolerance and wondering why he does not apply it to himself.

The answer, which they will not be slow to realise, is that the Pope condemns intolerance in the Communists and the Muslims and in other human groups because they are merely human. He does not condemn intolerance in himself because he is the mouthpiece of God; and he is not merely permitted, he is obliged, by virtue of his office, to persecute error wherever he finds it.

The Pope's statement on the World Day of Peace encapsulates the dilemma of any good-hearted religious man, whether he is a Catholic or a Hindu or a Muslim or a Protestant. A truly religious man, I once heard a Greek Orthodox bishop declaim in a sermon, is one who has sufficient faith to persecute others for their religious errors. Thus it is that while good and religious people (and I do not doubt the Pope's goodness) will frequently deplore the narrow-mindedness and intolerance of those who wish to persecute them, they reserve the right to coerce and attack those whom they would regard as heretics. Even, on occasion, they would consider it their duty to kill them.

'Surely, Mr Paisley,' I remember a Prime Minister saying on a television programme, 'you must realise that we are all children of God – whether we are Catholics or Protestants.'

'You, Mr Callaghan,' replied the leader of the strangely named Free Presbyterian Church of Ulster, 'have not read your Bible. Some of us are children of God, and others are children of wrath.'

Quite so. Crowns and thrones may perish; Prime Ministers rise and wane, but the Church of Paisley constant will remain. He was quite right. This is the Biblical teaching. The Old Testament is a handbook which justifies the killing and suppression of a lot of semitic tribes by the one semitic tribe which happens to have been chosen by God. The New Testament creates the New Israel, and provides a handbook for future Christians to treat heretics and infidels as, in ancient times, the Hebrews treated the Hivites, the Perizzites, the Canaanites, the Amorites, *et al.* These are what the Holy Father has rightly called 'history's painful lessons': crusades, religious wars, inquisitions, persecutions, burnings, bombings. No one would accuse the Reverend Ian Paisley, who once held a rally at which all loyal servants of the Gospel were asked to wave revolvers over their heads as an indication of what they thought of the Anglo-Irish Agreement, of the very slightest criminal tendency in himself. But there are many in the Province of Northern Ireland who are prompted by a similar devotion to the liberties of the Reformation to believe that there is nothing sinful in shooting Roman Catholics. Perhaps among the ranks of the IRA there are fewer religious fanatics than there once were, but the occasional gun-running priest still makes his appearance in the courts, hotly contesting extradition orders and reminding us of what it used to be like in the days when bishops blessed the tricolour and Catholic churches on both sides of the Irish channel held novenas of prayer for the success of the Republican terrorist campaigns. As I write these words, Iranians are being killed or bundled into jail for failing to follow the Qur'an according to the Ayatollah's peculiar specifications, Hindus are butchering Muslims in the streets of Delhi and Sikhs are rioting in the Punjab. Saddam Hussein is too busy bombing his own Kurdish rebels to recall that the Mother of All Battles was to have been blessed by Allah. Back home, Conservative politicians assert that it is perfectly right to thank God for the Allied victory. Behind the

Iron Curtain, Catholics and Orthodox are celebrating their new-found freedom from their Communist oppressors by making openly vicious tirades against the Jews, whom they blame for all the calamities which have befallen Holy Russia since the Revolution. Israeli soldiers, the while, are gunning down Muslim rioters (some of them children) outside the Holy Places in Jerusalem, while in Beirut, Christian militiamen are demonstrating the love of Christ towards their Muslim and Druse compatriots with howitzers, grenades and machine-guns. Onward Christian soldiers, marching as to war.

Now, most good religious people would wish to insist that religion is an essentially peaceable thing, and that all these atrocities, committed in the name of religion or with its blessing, are wicked aberrations. Salman Rushdie, who has surprised us all by announcing his conversion to Islam, would presumably wish us to believe that Allah is all-merciful, even though his servants the ayatollahs and mullahs are sometimes the reverse of merciful. Christians, Hindus, Sikhs, Shintoists, Parsees, Scientologists, Mormons would probably all wish to reiterate that they worship a God of Peace, and that the love of the human race is a cardinal doctrine of their faith. Although this argument is about as convincing as

9

the plea that Rottweilers make friendly family pets if they are only treated in the right way, or that no harm results from experimenting with heroin if you only take it in sufficiently mild doses, religious people can nearly always be sure of a tolerant hearing when they say it. We are so frightened of offending the religious sensibilities of other people that we do not like to ask them the awkward question. Why does so much unhappiness and bloodshed and conflict occur in the name of religion if it is so essentially good and peaceable a thing? Why has it always been so, and why does it continue to be so, even in these enlightened modern days when the Pope himself condemns 'the excesses of intolerance'? Surely, it needs to be said that all this evil does not stem from a perversion of religion but from religion itself, from pure religion and undefiled? It stems from the religious person's belief in God and his belief in absolutes. 'Think not,' said Christ, 'that I came to send peace on earth: I came not to send peace, but a sword.'

The decent, rational person, trying to make up his mind about some moral or social issue, will recognise that for the most part, he is floundering about in the dark. He will not hope to be certain of very much, and he will not begin to believe that what he thinks to be right for himself, or right for his society at this particular juncture of history, will be right always and everywhere for all men and women. But this is where the rational man differs from the religious man. The religious believer must believe in the universal applicability of his moral judgments as a rational consequence of his belief in God. God has spoken and revealed His will quite uniquely, through the tablets of the law on Mount Sinai, or on the golden plates which descended from Heaven to Joseph Smith the founder of the Mormons, or in the Qur'an, or through the promise given by Christ to St Peter that he would guide the Catholic Church into all truth. This belief defies argument from those who would wish to apply to it the ordinary standards of reason. No one who merely wished to be guided by common sense, or by simple kindness, would suggest that women living in shanty towns in South America should be denied the chance to practice contraception. But if God founded a Church, and if the Head of that Church says that contraception is in all circumstances sinful, then there can be no rational argument about the matter. The fact that these women are made to die appalling and humiliating deaths in their pathetic makeshift shelters cannot alter a divine decree. Similarly, if God decrees that a novelist deserves to die for something which he has written in a work of fiction, then it is not for imams or mullahs of a more kindly disposition than the Ayatollah to gainsay the words of the Deity.

The religious position offers its adherents the uniquely tempting satisfaction of giving a divine sanction to all their personal whims and prejudices. It is thus the most insidious vehicle for the abuse of power, whether by popes or by ayatollahs, over their credulous flocks; just as, in the private sphere of families and schools, it can be used by individuals to tyrannise over other people. 'I think' has been translated into 'God says'. A good illustration of the working of the religious mind occurs in the letters of J. R. R. Tolkien when he is discussing his friend C. S. Lewis's views of marriage. In a rare moment of tolerance, Lewis, in a wireless broadcast, had said, 'I'd be very angry if the Mohammedans tried to prevent the rest of us from drinking wine'; and he had gone on to argue that the Christian view of marriage was analogous. Christians had every right to uphold their own strictly monogamous principles, but no right to impose their views on non-Christians. Christian marriage, by Lewis's argument, should be confined to church. Those who did not share these views should be allowed to marry in registry offices and, if they so desired, to get divorced.

Not so, replied Tolkien. 'No item of compulsory Christian morals is valid *only for Christians.*' (My italics.) Divorce is contrary not merely to the rules of the Church but to the law of God which was decreed for the entire human race. It would be just as unlawful, by Tolkien's argument, for an atheist to obtain a divorce as for a Christian. Tolkien's position is perfectly logical, though not everyone will find it attractive. One finds it, in some shape or form, upheld by all those thoroughgoing super-naturalist Christians who intervene in areas of public life. They argue not from the point of view that, in a pluralist society, their voice deserves to be heard as much as anyone else's, but rather, that in a benighted and Godless society they have the duty to speak God's word and tell the rest of us how we should be thinking or behaving. The fact that, in Western society, very many people no longer have any formal religious allegiance does not alter the view that 'no item of Christian morals is valid only for Christians'.

Such figures are often somewhat selective in their presentation of Christian ethics to the rest of us, it is true. They tend to be more interested in sex than the rest of us. Mrs Mary Whitehouse is never slow to nose out pornographic scenes from books or films which many of us have never even heard of, though I have never once heard her say that her Christian conscience was scandalised by the activities of the Stock Exchange or the building societies who disregard Christ's injunction to lay up treasures not on earth but in heaven. A similar lack of restraint is found in another figure who increasingly attracts the limelight, that self-appointed defender of evangelical Christianity the Reverend Tony Higton.

Some evangelical Christians felt it their duty to circulate a copy of the *News of the World* to members of the General Synod of the Church of England, drawing their attention to an item concerning a much respected clergyman whose career was sub-sequently ruined. For those interested, it might be worth mentioning that the newspaper item merely recorded the admission of homosexual proclivities by the man concerned, and that the *News of the World* did not accuse him of any 'scandalous' behaviour. While recognising that these good people have the most admirable reasons for in-cluding that particular periodical among their devotional reading for Sunday morning, we might yet inquire as to what charitable motive they could possibly have for wishing to bring down shame and

ruin on one of their fellow human beings. The
answer is, of course, that they believe Almighty
God to share their own particular set of prejudices
about homosexuality.

Only mystics could guess what Jesus thought
about homosexuality, since his opinion on the
matter (if he had one) is not recorded in the Gos-
pels. Mr Higton's convictions about the subject,
bolstered by an aside of St Paul's in his Epistle to
the Romans, derive from an absolute identification
in his mind between his own views and those of
God. (St Paul also forebade women to pray with
their heads uncovered, but I very much doubt
whether Mr Higton throws out female worshippers
from his church if they listen to his sermons without
first arraying themselves in a hat or a mantilla.)
More recently, Mr Higton has been in the news
for denouncing the Queen, who apparently attends
an annual 'multi-faith' service, held in Westminster
Abbey on 'Commonwealth Day'. For those of us
who believe the Commonwealth is a fiction largely
existing in the mind of the monarch, there would
seem little harm in this annual religious expression
of her quasi-imperial dream. Mr Higton, however,
who is more rigorous in his approach to such
things, believes that the Head of the Established
Church should not be lifting up her voice in prayer

in the company of Sikhs, Brahmins, Muslims and Roman Catholics. She should insist upon a Protestant service and urge them all to be converted to Protestantism. The reason for this must be that Mr Higton's God is a Protestant God, just as J. R. R. Tolkien's God was a Catholic God and the Ayatollah's Allah is a Shia Allah.

The liberal Christian and, no doubt, the liberal Jew, can stand back from all this and acknowledge that when religious people use absolutist language, they are in fact worshipping projections of their own prejudices. The reason that people like Mr Higton and Mrs Whitehouse find God such a reassuring figure is that He is a mirror-image of themselves. But, say the liberals, God is not like that at all. The true God is ... well, He is rather a liberal: tolerant of homosexuality, extremely open-minded about multi-faith services, always on the side of peace and moderation, and in political matters earnestly occupying the middle ground. All that the liberals are doing when they tell us about the true God is removing an image of the Pope or Mrs Whitehouse and replacing it with an image of themselves. When their more cherished ideals are challenged, such liberals can reveal themselves to be just as intolerant as the most die-hard Muslims or Catholics. In the Church of England at the moment there are strong moves afoot to secure the ordination of women to the priesthood. Large numbers in that church are opposed to the measure, and large numbers are in favour. The liberals who are in favour of women priests have behaved with conspicuous intolerance towards those who disagree with them. They have ensured that Anglican priests who are opposed to the ordination of women stand almost no chance of promotion. They have labelled these opponents of theirs as fuddy-duddy, emotional inadequates. And why? Because, they insist, it is not a purely secular matter. They do not say that as a matter of justice, women should be allowed to be priests just as they can be doctors or judges or Prime Ministers. There would be some logic in that. They say, instead, that it is the will of God.

How do these religious people read the mind of God? How do they know what He is thinking? They can't. They merely use the word 'God' to reinforce their prejudices, and they then make universalist claims for their prejudices. Henceforward, they do not believe that they are expressing their own point of view; they are expressing God's. They are not content to tell us that Christians should refrain from, let us say, divorce or homosexuality. They wish to say that no one should practice these things, because they are contrary to the laws of Christ. The same applies to their views of artistic censorship, abortion, and more or less any other subject you care to mention. Sooner or later, someone will quote Dostoevsky to the effect that if God did not exist, anything would be permitted and that religion is the linch-pin of public morality. Unless people are given a reason for behaving well, it is argued, they will behave badly. That is the inheritance of original sin. It is only the dread of offending God which would prevent us all from turning into thieves, killers and fornicators on the grand scale.

In fact, the precise opposite of the Dostoevskyan tag is true. If goodness is good, then it will attract, and be pursued, for its own sake, and not because it has anything to do with religion. It never seems to occur to religious people that all through the centuries when religious belief was almost universal (including a belief in hell), the human race went on blaspheming and fornicating and thieving and killing, just as much as they do today. Nor would religious people be prepared to recognise that religion has certainly never made anyone a morally better person, and it has made most of its adherents worse. One of the strange and rather attractive features of modern life is how highly kindness and generosity are valued. Of course it can be sickening when pop stars or other public luminaries make displays of their charitable endeavours, but it remains true that charity and unselfishness are very widely valued for their own sake. Different generations invent or reinvent their own cardinal sins. In the generation now aged sixteen to twenty-five, I should say (to judge from my acquaintances in this age group) that the cardinal sins were racism and cruelty to animals. One can laugh at the earnestness which this sometimes produces, but on the whole it makes life pleasanter rather than the reverse, particularly if you happen to be either a fox or a human being of Afro-Caribbean descent. The impulses to 'feed the world', cherish its wildlife, to make life more bearable for ethnic or other 'minorities' are manifest and palpable among enormous numbers of young people today. I do not think these impulses are motivated by religious feelings of any kind. In empirical terms, it is simply untrue that when religion is discarded, the human race starts to behave very badly or to think cruel and unkind thoughts. Nor do I believe that the young 'undesirables' in our society, of whom there are so many – oiks, football hooligans, drug abusers, etc. – would be any better if to their other inadequacies was added a strong dose of God.

But, you might ask, why am I saying all this?

Does it even need to be said? Is it not what so many of us – us who buy or read CounterBlast pamphlets – know already?

I am not sure that it is. Religion, far from shrinking away, as our parents' generation believed that it would, is making a come-back, and that is bad news for the human race. I write as one who used to be religious, and who knows all the lure and the ecstasy and the joy of religion from the inside. I am still of a strongly religious temperament. I can never walk by the sea-shore, nor read Wordsworth, nor listen to Beethoven without feeling that 'there are more things in heaven and earth' than are dreamt of in a purely materialist view of things. But I am frightened by what happens when people of like mind or temperament get together and start to fashion these vague impulses of piety, these feelings of nameless humility before the mystery of things, into religious doctrines, party rules. I am totally convinced of the truth of Wittgenstein's words that whereof we cannot speak, we must be silent. There is a world of difference between a silent acknowledgment of the mystery and trumpeting religious fatuities in the ears of our fellow men. I have therefore decided quite consciously to eschew any religious allegiance. Cardinal Manning is said to have signed the pledge not because he was in any danger of abusing alcohol himself but because of the damage which he could see it doing in all the poorer districts of London. By a similar token, I feel that responsible persons, when religious impulses seize them, should 'commune in their own chambers and be still', and should resist the impulse to join any sect, group or church to promote their point of view. My pamphlet is devoted to the contention that religion in societies does more harm than good. You could, if you chose, view this pamphlet as an open letter to my old school-friend Salman Rushdie who is allying himself to one of the great world religions at the very point when I have become most certain that I wish to disassociate myself from another. Or you could view it as a comment on the present state of the blasphemy laws in England, and the debate about whether they should be abolished or whether they should be extended to non-Christian religions such as the Muslims or the Moonies. Or you could simply think of it as a profoundly conservative discovery – that Voltaire's motto is still as valid today as it was 200 years ago when he contemplated the damage done by superstition and religious bigotry: *Écrasez l'infame!*

It is not as if we were discussing a small minority of cranks who are incapable of doing harm to anyone. At this moment, it is said that over four fifths of the population of the United States of America are practising Christians, or have known the experience of being Born Again. In the United Kingdom the numbers of such 'born again' Christians must be much smaller, but these numbers are increasing. They will receive a tremendous boost now that one of their number has become the Archbishop of Canterbury.

Whereas wishy-washy Anglicans are frequently castigated in the popular press for their scepticism about such matters as the Virgin Birth, the evangelical party are widely saluted for their uncomplicated credulity. This can involve some curious mental gymnastics for those caught up in the evangelical experience. Some years ago, I attended one of their churches in London. It was the usual evangelical story. A few years earlier, when the vicar arrived in the place, there was a tiny congregation. Now they found difficulty in squeezing 700 worshippers into the place on a Sunday. For some reason, this sort of religion makes a great appeal to doctors and nurses, and on the Sunday when I went there were a large number of medics or medical students in the congregation. The sermon was extremely long and, like all the evangelical sermons which I have ever heard, it was about St

Paul's Epistle to the Romans, a favourite text. In the course of this homily, the preacher looked down at his flock and seriously alluded to the 'fact' that Abraham's wife Sarah had given birth to Isaac when she was over ninety years old. 'If someone came to your hospital and said that his ninety-year-old wife was about to give birth to a baby, you would think he was mad,' said the preacher. 'But that is what happened.' The man was not laughed at. They sat there and listened indulgently – the doctors, nurses, stockbrokers, lawyers, city merchants, teachers and bankers who made up the congregation. He was quite right. If, in ordinary life, they were told the story of an old woman of ninety becoming pregnant, they would dismiss it as an absurdity. But because the story was in the Bible, they were being asked to believe that it was literally true, and I do not doubt that the high proportion of those present did believe it.

All religions delight in such stories, and all religious people find themselves having to believe in six impossible things before breakfast. Sophisticated believers say that they do not believe in the literal truth of such tales, but only in the inner truth which they symbolise. For example, they do not believe that Sarah was literally ninety years old, but that we should all, like Sarah, put our trust in God and He will bring surprising things to pass in our lives. In my experience, however, this sort of religion is much rarer than the literalist or 'fundamentalist' variety. For example, I have asked many Roman Catholics if they really believe that the Virgin Mary, rather than dying in the normal way, arose into the clouds, body and soul, and was 'assumed' into heaven. They nearly always say that they accept and believe this doctrine without difficulty. This shows me that where matters of faith are concerned, the critical faculty goes to sleep. However intelligent the believer may be, he or she becomes totally passive in their approach to religious authority. This is surely a terrifying phenomenon, for it is exactly the same human characteristic which allowed the quasi-religious cults of the politically irrational which sent the world mad in the 1930s – Nazism, and Stalinism. There can be no possible truth in the story of Sarah being ninety when she gave birth to Isaac, nor in the Assumption of Our Lady. They are folk-tales with no historical substance in them whatsoever. The fact that intelligent and independent-minded people are prepared to suspend their critical faculties and believe such stories in exchange for the satisfaction vouchsafed by a religious observance, shows us that Dostoevsky's Grand Inquisitor stalks the earth, doing business as usual. In the original 'poem' by one of the Brothers Karamazov, it will be remembered that the Inquisitor in sixteenth-century Spain comes face to face with a Stranger and realises that Christ has returned to the earth. He berates Christ, who is silent throughout their interview, for having offered the human race the free choice of the heart, and love, which was not what they wanted. What the human race craves, according to the Grand Inquisitor, are the very three things which Christ rejected in the Wilderness during his Temptations. 'We had a right to preach mystery,' says the Inquisitor, 'and to teach them that it is not free choice of the heart that matters, and not love, but the mystery which they must blindly obey, even setting aside their own conscience. And so we did. We corrected your deed and based it on miracle, mystery and authority. And mankind rejoiced that they were once more led like sheep, and that at last such a terrible gift that had brought them so much suffering, had been taken from their hearts.'

When one sees the Pope praying at the famous Marian shrines of the world, Czestochowa, Lourdes, Fatima or Knock, where the most fantastic and implausible stories are peddled concerning the miraculous appearances of the Virgin Mary, one feels dumb with amazement that a man who is so obviously intelligent can be so willing to play the role of the Grand Inquisitor, dishing out miracle, mystery and authority in such generous doses to the hungry multitudes. Similar displays of mass human credulity in something which is, by any rational standards, incredible, can be seen by switching on the television in the United States and witnessing the activities of the telly-evangelists. Some of the more notorious of these preachers are now safely behind bars, or living in modest retirement, their chicanery and charlatanism exposed. But there are plenty of them still in business, peddling salvation by credit card with all the shameless gusto of Chaucer's Pardoner. The crazier and less credible the doctrines of any religion, the more ravenously it will be gobbled up and believed by someone or another: witness the continuing growth of the Mormon church, both in America and Europe.

It could be said that one should live and let live. I am not advocating that it should become illegal to believe nonsense, should people so choose. If your next-door neighbour believed that pigs could fly, it would be simple politeness to smile and nod while he explained the reasons for his belief. If you discovered that a dozen people met each week in this man's house to swap sightings of flying pigs, you might feel there was some cause for concern. If you then found out that he belonged to a world-wide organisation, with a membership of millions, all of whom had either seen flying pigs, or believed in the accounts of those who had done so, you would be aware that some very strange phenomenon was at work.

The old adage used to be that 'twenty million Americans can't be wrong'. We know this to be a preposterous suggestion and that the odds on twenty million Americans being right about anything are almost inconceivably small. But numbers talk. And there is something sinister, in my view, about the fact that the professional Grand Inquisitors, the Billy Grahams, the Pope John Paul IIs, achieve such widespread courtesy outside the household of their faiths. Wherever these particular individuals go, they are greeted by heads of State; red carpets are rolled out at airports; and even heads of State who could not possibly share their beliefs, such as President Havel of Czechoslovakia or Mikhail Gorbachev, evidently feel that they ought to be polite to them, for the sake of gratifying the religious sensibilities of their fellow countrymen. That is real power.

It is interesting to note the insidious means by which the Grand Inquisitor's power is manifested.

It is a dual power: the power to console, and the power to inflame indignation. Both these sorts of power frighten those who are outside the household of faith into thinking that religious believers need to be treated with kid gloves and afforded privileges which are denied to the world at large. In my view it is a mistake for societies to give in to this fear, for reasons which I shall explain towards the close of this pamphlet.

But let me expand a little upon these two types of power. First, the Grand Inquisitor has the power to console. Once his medicine has been swallowed it does not matter that common sense flatly contradicts every word he says. The believer is in pursuit of something much more palatable and attractive than the truth: it is the feeling of being loved – 'Ransomed, healed, restored, forgiven, Who like me His praise shall sing?' Religious egotism is the most potent form of egotism that exists. It can swell and grow and take over the earth. It begins with the simple egotism of believing that the Creator of Earth and Sky is perpetually engrossed in your personal moods, prayers, sins and virtues, and that He has gone to the trouble of inventing special punishments for you if you deviate from His law by thought, word or deed. The egotism flowers into the conviction that God was so worried about your

28

sinfulness that He came to earth in human form and died a painful and humiliating public death as a sacrifice for your transgressions. Anyone who is capable of believing these things has placed themselves, and their relationship with the Almighty, at the very centre of the universe. The consolation is enormous, and it is not difficult in these circumstances to see how the Inquisitor's power to console – by promoting such beliefs – also has the power to whip up fierce feelings of indignation when the beliefs are questioned or attacked.

It will be seen at once, if my diagnosis of religious egotism is correct, why the religious person considers him or herself to enjoy special privileges in society. After all, he or she has been chosen out by Allah or Jehovah or Jesus as a special friend, so that those who offend the believer are already close to offending God.

At this point we come to the questions raised by the laws of blasphemy. Are such laws brought into existence in order to protect the feelings of believers, or are they to enforce an orthodox view of God? When Salman Rushdie was condemned to death by the Iranian religious leadership, I made a remark in a newspaper article to the effect that Western liberals did not understand what blasphemy was. They did not realise that in cultures where blasphemy is a reality, no punishment, not even death itself, could be too severe. I was immediately castigated – in the same paper – for having called for the death of Mr Rushdie, a ludicrous interpretation to place on my words, but it showed that those who did so (not, I think, liberals) had an equally hazy understanding of what blasphemy is. Islam, Judaism and Christianity have all, at various stages of their evolution, advocated the death penalty for blasphemy. 'We have a law, and by our law he ought to die', as the chief priests say of Jesus at the time of his trial. First century AD Pharisees, sixteenth-century Catholics sending heretics to the stake, and twentieth-century Muslims would all understand one another in this area. Since, for these people, God is really God, it is essential to worship Him and believe in Him aright, and for this cause they were, and are, prepared to enforce this doctrine by whatever means necessary, however cruel. It is for this reason that I began this pamphlet as I did with the view that the love of God is the root of all evil.

As a hangover from the days when England still burnt heretics, or, more modestly, cut off their ears for refusing to wear the surplice, or locked them in Bedford Gaol where they poured out their soul into melancholy prose works such as *The Pilgrim's*

Progress – as a relic from those days, we still have
a blasphemy law. The purpose of the law is not to
protect God – who needs no protection – but to
protect us from religious error. It has nothing whatsoever to do with the feelings, hurt or otherwise, of
orthodox religious believers. Ridley and Latimer
when they were led through the streets of Oxford
to be burnt at the stake were asked one more time
to recant their errors – which they nobly refused to
do. They were not asked to apologise for the deep
sense of hurt which they had inflicted upon Bloody
Mary or Cardinal Pole. Jesus and St Stephen were
not accused of having hurt the feelings of the High
Priests. They were condemned to die for blasphemy, pure and simple.

Knowing this as he does, the Grand Inquisitor
is still perfectly prepared to use the 'hurt feelings'
trick for stirring up trouble and wielding power.
After Salman Rushdie published *The Satanic Verses*,
a book which very few people have ever read, the
Muslim community of Bradford found themselves
being whipped up into frenzies of 'hurt' by their
local Inquisitors. Copies of the novel were heaped
on to burning pyres – a scene almost unknown in
England since the Reformation, almost unimagin-
able in the 'civilised' world. The rest, as they say,
is history. What was interesting, in all subsequent

debates, was the anxiety expressed by well-meaning Anglican bishops, Labour MPs, and *bien-pensant* observers of the scene, that the blasphemy law should be limited to the Christian God, rather than being extended to include Allah. The reason advanced for this ludicrous suggestion was simple. The Muslim community felt deeply hurt by Salman Rushdie's book, and therefore there ought to be some redress in the law which would prevent such groups from being deeply hurt in the future. Blasphemy, by this definition, has come to mean anything which could conceivably hurt a religious person, however touchy they might be, and however far-fetched and fatuous their views. The logical extension of such an idea would be that the 'blasphemy' law should be extended to make it impossible to make slighting remarks about the Moonies or the Scientologists, impossible to make jokes about Jehovah's Witnesses, impossible to express the serious disquiet which many of us might feel about the growth of intolerant religious groups within a supposedly pluralist society.

The price any of us pay for living in a pluralist society is that we must often come across views and opinions and lifestyles very different from our own. Some people might wish, precisely for this reason, that our society was not pluralist, and that everyone in England was white, Christian and Protestant. It is not so. And if we are to live peaceably together we must be prepared to make sacrifices.

This is something which the religious lobby resolutely refuses to accept. Mr Higton, castigating the Queen for worshipping with Muslims and Hindus, or Mrs Whitehouse, reviving the antiquated laws of blasphemy in order to prosecute *Gay News*, are arguing the same case for themselves as the Muslims of Bradford who burnt Salman Rushdie's book. And, as things stand at present in Great Britain, one sees that the Muslims have a cause of grievance. The Head of State is indeed the Head of the Established Church. Christianity is the official religion of the country, even though the greater part of his citizens are not practising Christians. And there remains a law of blasphemy which forbids you to say disrespectful things about Jesus but allows you to say what you like about the Prophet. In addition, the House of Lords contains Anglican bishops – *ex officio* – and the former Chief Rabbi – who sits as a Life Peer, in deference to Mrs Thatcher's Finchley constituents – but no mullahs, no Hindu priests, no cardinals, no representatives of the Sikhs.

If you follow the line taken by old-fashioned

Christians such as Mr Higton, it would be possible to argue that those who come to live in a Christian country must conform to Christian laws, Christian rules, Christian institutions. Common sense and natural justice, however, makes it impossible to follow this line. Mr Higton and his like are – we might thank whatever Gods there be – still in a minority in this country. It is absurd to pretend that Britain is a 'Christian' country and it gives far too high a public profile to religion and its trappings. If the non-Christians in Britain were all agnostic, this probably would not matter very much. But the presence in our society of large groups of actively religious non-Christians makes it necessary to revise the whole way in which, as a society, we view the religious question – in terms of law, in terms of educational arrangements, in terms of national pageantry, etc.

The Rushdie affair has shown us that it is no longer possible to find a consensus. Where religion is concerned, there is no such thing as a consensus. It is only those who have no religion, or whose religion has become so intertwined with post-war liberal kindliness as to have become secularised, who can continue to dream of a peaceful 'multi-faith', pluralist society. For the truly religious people in our midst, such an idea is anathema.

Witness the fuss they create if, instead of formal religious instruction in our schools, the old 'R.I.' lessons become exercises in Comparative Religion, in which the children learn, for example, the myths from the Bhagavad Gita, the various ritual customs of the Jewish liturgical year, and so forth. These comparative religion lessons have great interest for the children, and great charm for agnostic grown-ups. But for those who actually believe that God has spoken uniquely to the human race, they are worse than nonsensical; they are blasphemous. If you actually believe in the Qur'an, or the Catholic catechism, or the Orthodox Jewish faith, there could be few things more offensive than your child being taught that the core of your creed, the very thing by which you live, is no more than a sociological phenomenon. Catholics are Catholics because they believe that the Word was made flesh, and dwelt among us, and continues to dwell among us in the person of the Church. Muslims are Muslims because they believe that God has spoken through His Prophet and taught the human race how to live through the pages of the Qur'an. Jews are Jews because they were born Jews, but also because they believe that God has given to their race a unique spiritual burden and insight. Their beliefs are all strongly held, and they are all incompatible with one another, and incompatible with Anglicanism, Mormonism, Buddhism, and all the other creeds upheld by separate individuals and families within our society.

So strongly are religious beliefs held that it has been considered necessary, since the last century, to have within our midst separate schools to cater for the different religious minorities. Although all the educational reforms in Great Britain since the 1960s have been secularist in character, they have inherited from the Victorians – who first began to set up special schools for Jews, Catholics, Methodists and others – the liberal notion that the State should respect the tender consciences of religious minorities by this encouragement of separatism. In so doing, we have, as a society, stored up trouble for ourselves. Part of the trouble has sprung from the good example of the Jews, who have never, so far as I am aware, done any harm to any society in which they have lived their religiously separate lives. The Jewish approach to the life of faith has been an ideal mixture of stand-offishness and tolerance. 'Let us follow our faith, and our laws,' they have said, 'and educate our children in the way that we think best. And we shall in turn be good citizens.' So they have proved to be.

But in the religious life, analogies do not work.

Other religious groups can say, 'Look at the Jews. They have special schools. They have their own religion. Why can't we?' The great difference between Jews and most other religious people, of course, is that they do not wish to make any converts. Jesus, in this regard as in so many others, was typically Jewish when he said that he had no interest in Gentiles, no wish to convert them, no desire even to speak to them unless they spoke to him. He was sent, he said, 'to the lost sheep of the House of Israel.' In any society where there are significant numbers of Jews, therefore, they do not cause disruption. It could be said, and by the more despondent and angry Jews of my generation it is sometimes said, that historically the Jews have not been disruptive enough: they have been too tolerant, too ready to allow the Gentiles to encroach upon their rights, violate their laws, and even to persecute them. Certainly, however, except in a very few cases of dotty Jewish extremists in New York and Jerusalem, you never come across the Jews behaving in a socially disruptive manner. You do not find them making public protests because the Gentile society in which they live is offensive to them. The vast majority of British Jews, for instance, send their children to Gentile schools, and there is little apart from diet which sets the

37

average British Jew apart from his Gentile fellow citizens.

In these circumstances, one sees the absurdity of pretending that the Muslims can be 'treated just like the Jews', since they have never at any stage behaved just like the Jews. They belong to a religion which, like Christianity, makes universalist claims. The good Catholic believes that the human race, all of it, should be Catholic. The good Mormon likewise. And the good Muslim believes that all men and women should accept that there is but one God and Muhammad is His Prophet.

Societies which have been wholly and exclusively governed by these religious groups have always, historically, been intolerant of other faiths. The non-Mormon in Salt Lake City, the non-Catholic in Franco's Spain or de Valera's Ireland (where it was impossible by law to buy a contraceptive or a copy of Ireland's greatest twentieth-century prose work) suffered the same sort of exclusion as non-Muslims in Saudi Arabia, where visiting troops from the West, ready to lay down their lives for the Arab emirates in a war with Iraq, were not even allowed to celebrate Christmas.

When these things are borne in mind, it will be seen why a liberal, pluralist society such as Great Britain cannot treat the Muslims as it treats the

Jews. There are many modern works of literature which are highly offensive to the Jews – for example, the words of that brilliant old rogue, of whom I once wrote a biography, Hilaire Belloc. Even his *Cautionary Verses* for children bristles with anti-Jewish prejudice. There has never been an occasion, so far as I recall, when the Chief Rabbi organised public burnings of Belloc's works, or when my life was threatened for trying to paint a fair portrait of the old monster, or when the office of Belloc's publishers had to be guarded twenty-four hours round the clock by security guards and sniffer dogs.

The Rushdie affair made it clear why pluralism and liberalism no longer work. It is because religious minorities will not accept their status as minorities. They do not, of course, all wish to kill people who disagree with them; but they do believe that they have special privileges and rights, merely because of the strength and passion of their religious convictions. I believe that the time has come for the government and society at large to tell them that they do not. If we go on saying that Muslims and Catholics and Mormons and Anglicans and any other religious group we like to name deserve these special privileges, we shall have a ceaseless repetition of the Rushdie affair. We shall have a new blasphemy law, making it impossible to blaspheme anyone's God – and this in practice will mean that it will merely be illegal to tread on anyone's toes. If religion could be shown to have brought light and joy and peace into the world, there might be a case for such measures being passed through Parliament. Since it has consistently done the opposite, we are mad to consider granting it any further concessions.

Muslims and others are right to suggest that it is unfair, in a pluralist society, to have a blasphemy law which only applies to the Christian God. But that is an argument not for extending the blasphemy law but for scrapping it altogether. Catholics are right to say that, since they form the majority of churchgoing Christians in Great Britain, it is unfair for the Church of England to be 'the Established Church', with bishops sitting in the House of Lords, and the Queen and her heirs obliged by law to be Protestant. But that is not an argument for having cardinals in the House of Lords. It is an argument for disestablishing the Church of England, and abolishing the concept of a State religion. Muslims and others are right to say that it is unfair, when there are so many schools specially maintained, with State aid, for Jews, Catholics and Anglicans, that there should not be more money put aside for special Muslim schools, in which the girls and boys are taught separately, and the girls are trained to think of themselves as a sub-species who do not really need or deserve an education at all. But this is not in fact an argument for the State creating more Muslim schools. It is an argument for the State withdrawing all funds from religiously affiliated schools, and only having secular schools. The only way in which we can hope to eliminate religious tension from our society is to cease to be, or to pretend to be, a religious society.

I am aware that there are many benign and intelligent figures who think quite differently about this matter. One of the most benign, and most intelligent, is the Chief Rabbi who delivered last year's Reith Lectures on BBC Radio 4. In the course of those well balanced and attractive discourses, Rabbi Jonathan Sacks reflected on many of the subjects which have been my concern in this pamphlet, and reached some of the same conclusions. 'Twenty years ago,' he said, 'it seemed as if religion had run its course in the modern world. Today a more considered view would be that its story has hardly yet begun . . . Even in Britain, I suspect that we will hear more about it in the future than for a long time past. There will be the Decade of Evangelism; anguished voices within Islam; periodic tension in Catholicism . . .' Where the Rabbi and I differ is in seeing these developments, which are certainly occurring, as signs of life. I feel as if he were an intelligent surgeon, surveying the X-rays of his patient, the body politic, and noticing signs of growth, where I only see signs of growths – cancerous and deadly growths which can only lead to discord and disharmony. The Decade of Evangelism, if it works, will mean a Decade of the Reverend Tony Higton, spreading his hateful and intolerant creed among the impressionable young, a decade of Mrs Whitehouse and her like advertising her self-righteous and unpleasant views, and making life difficult for those, such as homosexuals and unmarried mothers, whose lives are often quite difficult enough already. The 'periodic tensions' in Catholicism which the Rabbi observes with such a tolerant and kindly eye will mean a decade in which more priests and professors are suspended from their teaching offices for saying what they think, and more South American women die because they are not allowed to use the contraceptive pill. The mind boggles at what blessings will be shed upon the human race by the 'anguished voices within Islam.'

I want to say to the Chief Rabbi: the Jews are quite exceptional people, and you should not judge the rest of the human race by your own exceptional standards. Has not the history of your religion taught you that these people, of whom you speak so kindly, the Muslims and the Christians, are not to be trusted? True, they share your belief in a good and merciful God; true, they subscribe to the idea, never more sublimely expressed than in your own Scriptures, that we must love our neighbours as ourselves; but it never quite works out like that. One of your fellow Jews whose name was Saint Paul and who, by Jewish standards, went off the rails, once wrote, 'The good that I would, I do not; the evil I would not, that I do.' He had enunciated a profound truth about the religious tragedy, but he had not seen that the essence of this tragedy was religion itself. It was not the cure which he, and you, and I, and millions of religious people throughout history have sought. It was the disease itself.

Looking to the future, the Rabbi admitted that 'the question will be whether they [that is, the world religions] can be revived without the intolerances that once made religion a source of prejudice as well as pride.' I have said enough in this pamphlet to make it clear why I believe such an aspiration impossible and unrealistic. The Rabbi set out to consider the Enlightenment belief that sooner or

later religion, that moribund combination of superstition and deceit, would die, to be replaced by
more rational attitudes to life. Religions do die, or
seem to be dying, but they never quite expire. And
he points to 'the surprising persistence of faith'.
When you think about it, is it so very surprising?
The Enlightenment supposed that it was conquer-
ing superstition, but it actually replaced old
superstitions with new ones. The Encyclopaedists
thought that they could conquer all that was least
desirable in human nature and human society by
the pursuit of Reason, and plunged France and
most of Europe into the Terror – an unparalleled
period of unreason and anarchy. Marx worshipped
Justice, with the passion of one of the eighth-
century Jewish prophets. He believed that it must
come to pass as a result of the determinist economic
laws which had replaced, in his imagination, the
eternal Providence of God. The result, in the countries where his theories were put into practice, was
bloodshed and anarchy worse than that caused by
Reason in eighteenth-century France. Freud, that
other great prophet of the Enlightenment, gazed
into the bottomless pits of unreason which lie in the
human soul and thought that it might be possible, if
patients were treated to sufficiently rigorous analy-
sis and cure, to rid the world of the human

propensity to fantasise, the propensity to protect ourselves with untruths as a weapon against the darkness within. I think that most psychiatrists, and certainly most observant students of the human condition, would agree that this ideal is impossible. Reason, justice and sanity are, it would seem from history, less attractive to people *en masse* than violence, chaos, muddle and folly. There is no such thing as collective virtue, only individual virtue. It is a well attested human phenomenon that a group of wise men and women, when formed into a committee, start to form foolish resolutions. Swell the committee to a crowd, and it becomes capable of madness. It is this fact to which the apparently reasonable sages of the Enlightenment were so blind; and it is this fact which has kept the Grand Inquisitor in business for thousands of years, feeding the masses with the nonsense for which they are actually hungry. When politicians usurp the Grand Inquisitor's role, they are nearly always crude enough to show their hand, so that the essential ugliness of their game – as in the case of Hitler or Stalin – is apparent from the beginning. The insidious quality of religion – and herein lies the genius of Dostoevsky's story – is that it beguiles the human race – not with evil aspirations but with good ones. The Judaeo-Christian tradition, particularly when infused with the spirit of Platonism, offered to men and women a chance to pursue the good life through a series of sublime imperatives: to die to oneself in order to live; to love neighbour as one loves oneself; to love good for its own sake; to care for the poor, the sick, the needy, the imprisoned as if they were the embodiment of Christ himself.

Religions, by claiming these ideals to themselves, blaspheme against them. They posit two great lies. The first lie is that of miracle and mystery. They suggest that you can only pursue the good if you subscribe to stories and doctrines against which the reason justly rebels. As if there were not enough mysteries and miracles in religion's box of tricks from the past, they are ever-anxious to invent and discover more – as we witness every year, with the invention of apparitions of the Blessed Virgin in the Yugoslavian skies, or mysterious answers to prayer as a result of phone-ins on American television. The second lie is that these ideals – dressed up in theological language as being in a state of grace or of friendship with God – are only attainable if you belong to a group, a church, to 'the blessed company of all faithful people' as defined by Islam or Catholicism.

It is precisely because the human hunger for

good is so strong that it can so easily be turned to evil. Only a small number of perverts would ever have voted for Hitler if they had known the full extent of his sadistic and destructive world programme. The Germans who voted him into power and attended his rallies were attracted at first by good things – the prospect of full employment and social order and the restoration of national dignity – and they were seduced by the hypnotism of his mass rallies into believing that his movement would bring them to pass. Thirties leftists are mocked today for their desire to support Stalinism, but they did so because of the good which it offered – the destruction not merely of fascism, but of poverty and of injustice. The great majority of religious people are, similarly, drawn to the organised religions of the world by the same impulses which move all human beings when confronting the mystery of things – in landscape, in music, in the experiences of love and loss. They do not join these religions, or remain in the religion of their parents, primarily because they believe the fantastical claims and doctrines, but because they believe in the ideals, and they believe that all these good things will be lost unless, like frightened children, they hold on to the ugly and evil things in their religion for fear of losing what they love. It is one of the more depressing features of the religious psyche that in time it comes positively to love the authoritarianism and spiritual bullying and intolerance and sheer bare-faced dishonesty which characterises the major world religions.

We cannot hope for a society in which formal organised religion dies out. But we can stop behaving as if it was worthy of our collective respect. We cannot hope for a world in which religious groups do not exercise moral blackmail by claiming 'profound hurt' whenever books, films, plays or journalism appear to which they happen to take exception. But we can do our best to ignore all such moral blackmail, and all the threats of ayatollahs, popes and mullahs by being as consistently and truthfully offensive as we can. We cannot stop the Pope appearing on his balcony and telling us how to think and behave, any more than we can stop *fatwa*s being issued from the Ayatollah. But we can do more than turn a deaf ear to them when they do so. We can cheer when their own people have the spirit to rebel against them, and we can boo whenever these religious bullies open their mouths. It is true that they are frightening, particularly when they issue threats of death. But it is a definition of cowardice that we should feel frightened of saying boo to a goose. The Pope is a very powerful goose.

The Ayatollah Khameini is an even greater goose. Mrs Whitehouse is a minor goose. The Reverend Tony Higton and Ian Paisley are noisy little ganders. Boo, boo, boo to them all.

About the Author

A. N. WILSON has written biographies of John Milton, Hilaire Belloc, Tolstoy and C. S. Lewis. He is an acclaimed novelist and a prolific journalist.

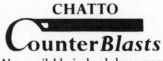

CHATTO

Counter*Blasts*

Also available in bookshops now:-

If you want to join in the debate, and if you want to know more about Counter*Blasts*, the writers and the issues, then write to:

Random Century Group, Freepost 5066, Dept MH, London SW1V 2YY